Dedication

To my Lord and Savior Jesus Christ. I offer back to You the gifts You have given me as a sacrifice of praise. I will do my best to be Your herald and encourage others to do the same.

This book is dedicated to my parents, Maurice and Betty Gentry, for their lifetime of sacrifices, countless hours of prayer, endless devotion, and firm belief in my giftings. How blessed I am to be your child, and how blessed Chad and I are to still have you with us.

Acknowledgments

Thank you to my husband, Adam, for being my calm center, my covering, my cheerleader, my critical thinker, and my life partner. I love you endlessly and am grateful to be on this *Herald* journey together.

Thank you to my brother, Chad, for all your guidance and advice, for blazing a trail for *Herald* to exist, and for your devoted friendship throughout our entire lives. There exists no better brother or friend than you.

Introduction

What an honor to have you join me on my *Herald* journey!

I wrote this book to provide an immersive *Herald* experience, where you can deep dive into the stories behind the songs on my *Herald* album (called "Reflections"), read the Bible verses that anchor each song, view the paintings that are woven into the *Herald* story, and listen to each song using the QR code provided.

There are eight chapters in this book—one for each song, and I recommend that you take it one chapter at a time. I've taken great care to make this a friendly format that is not overwhelming, and one that works well for both individual and group study.

Now, let me tell you a little about how *Herald* came to be...

Herald History

About two years ago I was feeling stuck and needed some direction. I asked the Lord, "Who am I to You? What do You have for me?" I knew what His Word says about my identity, and I had received all that, but I needed some specific direction. I wanted to dig deeper into my calling.

He answered right away. He said (not audibly, but very clearly in my head/heart), "You are my herald."

Well, that was unexpected. It was definitely not a word I was thinking about, so I knew it was the Lord. But I asked again, just to make sure I heard it right. He responded exactly the same way again, saying "You are my herald." And that was the end of the conversation. Simple and to the point, just how I prefer communication. (It's amazing how the Lord knows how to speak to us in exactly the way we can relate to best!)

Needless to say, this conversation stuck with me. I studied every definition of "herald" I could find and every instance where the word has been used, both in and outside of the Bible. From John the Baptist preparing the

way of the Lord to the herald angels declaring Christ's birth to the historical accounts of town criers shouting the news...it all came down to proclaiming and declaring, to being an instrument of truth and sharing important news.

After living with this word for a while, it started to feel like a familiar fit. But I still needed to figure out more specifically what to do with this "herald" calling that was uniquely me...

The *Herald* Album

I asked the Lord what He wanted me to do to be His herald. I basically said (I'm paraphrasing this time because I don't remember the exact words I asked, but this is close): "Okay, Lord. I'm on board with this herald thing. Of course I want to be Your herald. Of course I want to proclaim Your goodness, Your restoration, Your salvation, Your return...but what do You want me to do that specifically uses the talents You gave me?"

He responded quickly (again!), and said, "Do an album." That's all He said.

I'm not actually sure what I was expecting the Lord to tell me to do, but it was not that. I had no plans to record more music. I felt like that time had passed me by. So I proceeded to tell Him all the reasons why I didn't think it was a good idea. He simply said, again, "Do an album."

Well, long story short, I got on board with His plan and created an album of eight original songs. I named the project *Herald* to honor those conversations.

The *Herald* Paintings

During the time I was making the *Herald* album, I asked the Lord what else I could do to be His herald. I was sensing there was more but didn't know what. He said, "Paint," and began giving me images of sunsets. I hadn't painted anything substantial for quite a while, so this, too, was a surprise. To be honest, I was not excited about picking up a paintbrush again, because I didn't feel my abilities were adequate to create paintings that were "good enough" to offer to the Lord. I think it was in that moment that I realized I

didn't have to be "good enough," because I wasn't doing this on my own. He was co-creating with me. I just needed to be obedient.

I gathered up some old canvases and paints I had on hand and began interpreting the sunset images the Lord gave me as best I could. These are the images on the following pages, each one paired to a song on the *Herald* album. To me the sunsets signify His return, but I expect the images will speak to viewers differently, in personal ways, as art does. And I love that all eight pieces were created using upcycled materials, because it reminds me that He gives us renewed purpose and brings restoration to our lives in so many ways.

I pray the Lord speaks to you through the *Herald* experience—through words, songs, and images—and that you experience the peace and restoration that only He can give.

Foreword

There has never been another book like the one you are holding in your hands, because there has never been another artist who could produce such a book besides Kim Gentry Meyer. Think for a moment about all the Christian authors you admire. Hopefully, they are all well studied in Scripture and know how to reach into your moments of greatest despair and help you remember that the Lord is faithful. But of them all, how many could turn those scriptures into a song so that you can audibly hear God's message and drown out the Enemy's lies? And of the ones who could do both, how many could paint a colorful picture that enables your eyes to literally see that realm that your soul has now been able to touch? And even if you found another artist who could do all of those things, would they be able to summarize this journey for you and turn it into a prayer that is a heartfelt aroma, pleasing to the Lord? Likely not. But Kim Gentry Meyer has. This book is a true gift for all your senses, friend. Employ each one, then taste and see that the Lord is good.

Dr. Laura Harris Smith
Author, TV Host of *theTHREE*, Naturopathic Doctor

1
This Isn't Heaven

This Isn't Heaven

by Kim Gentry Meyer and Karl Anderson

Verse 1

Caught up in the life
We've worked hard to make
So busy with trying to win
We forget what's at stake

We live in the present
Focused just on today
Saying life is too short so step out
Leave it all on the stage

Pre-chorus/Bridge

What have we gained at the end of the day when it all fades away

Chorus

Why are we living like this is heaven
When this isn't heaven

Verse 2

All in on a lie
That says do as you please
There's no right and no wrong
There's just now
So keep living your dreams

Anchor scriptures

- Hebrews 13:14 For here we do not have an enduring city, but we are looking for the city that is to come.
- Philippians 3:20 But our citizenship is in heaven. And we eagerly await a Savior from there, the Lord Jesus Christ…
- Matthew 16:26 What good will it be for someone to gain the whole world, yet forfeit their soul?

Reflection

This song deals with how we can get so caught up in our daily lives, trying to "get ahead" and "climb the ladder," focusing on all the measures of success by which this life and others judge us and all the things that seem important in the moment (Verse 1). But when we step back, we realize none of it is that important. All the stuff, all the accolades…they will all fade away (Bridge).

I wrote this song to ask myself…*Why am I living like this is all there is? Why am I living like this is my permanent home? I'm just passing through this life, on my way to an eternal home that is infinitely better than my present reality. So why don't I put more focus there? Why don't I line up my thoughts, efforts, and resources accordingly?* As the Chorus I wrote asks, "Why are we living like this is heaven when this isn't heaven?" Writing this song prompted me to do an audit of how I spend my time, talent, and treasures and make some adjustments.

Questions

- What lyrics in this song stand out to you most? Why do you connect with them?
- Do you feel the pull between this world and heaven? Why do you think it's so easy to get caught up in the temporal and live like we're already home?

- What are some strategies you use to balance the demands of daily life with a focus on what one of the anchor scriptures above calls our "citizenship in heaven"? Does this song help you with this balance? Why or why not?
- How does the painting speak to you on this topic?

Prayer

Lord, give me wisdom and discipline to navigate this tension between now and eternity. Help me prioritize my time, talent, and resources so that they better align with Your Word, Your will, and what is to come. In Jesus' name, amen.

2

Mind of Christ

Mind of Christ

by Kim Gentry Meyer and Karl Anderson

Verse 1

I'm overwhelmed
In a world that's not for me
So hard to stay up
When my thoughts take me deep

It's like walking in a dark room
In the middle of the night
Feeling lost and lonely
Cause I can't find the lights

Chorus

I need the mind of Christ to come and cover me
I need the mind of Christ to come and set me free
This battle that I'm facing
Is not the earthly kind
Jesus come restore my peace of mind

Verse 2

I'm holding on
To the Truth I know is real
Who I am
Is more than how I feel

It's like waiting for the summer
In the middle of the snow
The cold feels like forever
But in springtime it goes

Bridge

The mind of the Spirit is life and peace
Darkness has no place in what the Son sets free

Anchor scriptures

- Ephesians 6:12 For our struggle is not against flesh and blood, but against the rulers, against the authorities, against the powers of this dark world and against the spiritual forces of evil in the heavenly realms.
- Romans 8:6 The mind governed by the flesh is death, but the mind governed by the Spirit is life and peace.
- Romans 12:2 Do not conform to the pattern of this world, but be transformed by the renewing of your mind.

Reflection

In my experience, discussions about mental health are still not commonplace, especially in the Christian community. I find this especially troubling since Scripture repeatedly highlights the battle for our minds and the importance of coming to Christ for continual renewal (Chorus).

I wrote "Mind of Christ" to shine a light on this topic and provide an opening for honest conversations. I even created a music video for this song to visually demonstrate the idea of coming out of darkness into the light by renewing our mind through prayer and reading God's Word (see QR code on lyrics page for link to the music video).

I have dealt with depression myself, so I can relate personally to the challenge of walking through darkness (Verse 1). While our journey out of this darkness can sometimes be gradual (Verse 2), I praise God that "...the mind of the Spirit is life and peace" and that "darkness has no place in what the Son sets free" (Bridge). I have found that being rooted in Scripture and praying daily for a Christ-like mind is foundational to walking through this life in peace.

I pray this song is a helpful tool in your own mental wholeness journey.

Questions

- Read through the anchor scriptures. Given this context, read the song lyrics again. What lyrics in this song stand out to you? Why do you relate to them most?
- Use the QR code on the lyrics page to watch the music video and visually experience the ministry of this song. Is there a part of the video that speaks to you in your own mental wholeness journey? What is it?
- Renewal takes time. Do you have strategies to renew your mind regularly? What are they? Does "Mind of Christ" suggest new ways to help you renew your mind?
- How does the painting speak to you on this topic?

Prayer

Heavenly Father, in the name of Jesus, through the power of the Holy Spirit, I ask that You renew my mind and fill it with Your peace. Help me prioritize coming to You for daily renewal. I claim the access I have to the freedom Jesus paid for, and I stand on Your promise that my mind can be renewed and that my life can be transformed. Amen.

If you are struggling with your mental health, don't wait to reach out. Here's a list of resources to help point you in a positive direction.

3

You'll Find Me There

You'll Find Me There

by Kim Gentry Meyer and Karl Anderson

Verse 1

When your prayers are more than habit
And My verses more than lines
When communion's more than kneeling
To take the bread and wine
You'll find Me there
You'll find Me there

Verse 2

When there's peace instead of slander
And you seek to understand
When you care for all creation
When you lend a helping hand
You'll find Me there
You'll find Me there

Verse 3

When the weight is on your shoulders
And the poor become your own
When you choose to love the haters
And you take the higher road
You'll find Me there
You'll find Me there

Verse 4

When your treasures bless My Kingdom
Instead of earthly gain
When your joy is found in serving
And you give instead of take
You'll find Me there
You'll find Me there

Anchor scriptures

- Galatians 5:22–23 But the fruit of the Spirit is love, joy, peace, forbearance, kindness, goodness, faithfulness, gentleness and self-control.
- Isaiah 1:17 Learn to do right; seek justice. Defend the oppressed. Take up the cause of the fatherless; plead the case of the widow.
- Ephesians 4:31–32 Get rid of all bitterness, rage and anger, brawling and slander, along with every form of malice. Be kind and compassionate to one another, forgiving each other, just as in Christ God forgave you.
- Philippians 2:3–5 Do nothing out of selfish ambition or vain conceit. Rather, in humility value others above yourselves, not looking to your own interests but each of you to the interests of the others. In your relationships with one another, have the same mindset as Christ Jesus.
- Galatians 6:2 Carry each other's burdens, and in this way you will fulfill the law of Christ.
- Hebrews 13:16 And do not forget to do good and to share with others, for with such sacrifices God is pleased.
- John 15:12 My command is this: Love each other as I have loved you.
- Proverbs 19:17 Whoever is kind to the poor lends to the LORD.
- Matthew 5:44 But I tell you, love your enemies and pray for those who persecute you.
- Luke 6:27–28 But to you who are listening I say: Love your enemies, do good to those who hate you, bless those who curse you, pray for those who mistreat you.

Reflection

I originally wrote the lyrics of this song as a poem and am honored to have been named a 2023 Woody Guthrie Poet for it. My goal was to explore social justice through a Biblical lens, using the fruit of the Spirit as guiding principles and breaking them down in each verse with examples. What an amazing measure they provide for examining the condition of the heart! As with everything I write, I endeavor to encourage, so while I know these lyrics can be challenging, I hope they also give you hope. They encourage me because they make me think about what's possible if we live out the fruit of the Spirit in our daily lives by practicing love, joy, peace, forbearance, kindness, goodness, faithfulness, gentleness, and self-control.

Questions

- Do you agree that the fruit of the Spirit are a good road map for living a compassionate and effective life for Christ? Why or why not?
- Which of the concepts mentioned in the lyrics align most with your own spiritual giftings? Which ones are the greatest challenge for you?
- There are so many rich scriptural references in this song. Do any of the anchor Bible verses above stand out to you in a new way after considering this song? If so, how?
- How does this song's painting speak to you?

Prayer

Lord, show me where I'm modeling the fruit of the Spirit well, and also where I'm not. I want to prioritize living the way these lyrics demonstrate. While the world judges success by vastly different metrics, I want to focus on living like Jesus. Open my eyes to see the opportunities around me to serve others. In Jesus' name, amen.

4
Remain in You

Remain in You

by Kim Gentry Meyer

Verse

What more is there
Than to breathe You in
And breathe You out
To feel Your presence
To seek Your will
To know without a doubt

Chorus

In You we live
In You we move
In You we find ourselves
We're found in You
In You we trust
Fear is removed
In You we find ourselves
We're found in You

Bridge

We remain in You
You remain in us
You are our shelter
In You we trust

Anchor scripture

- John 15:5 I am the vine; you are the branches. If you remain in me and I in you, you will bear much fruit; apart from me you can do nothing.

Reflection

This song focuses on the latter part of John 15:5—the part that says, "...If you remain in Me and I in you, you will bear much fruit..." I wanted to focus on this part because you typically hear the first part quoted—the part that says, "I am the vine; you are the branches." But the "remain in" part always speaks to me so deeply, too, so I wanted to further explore this idea of "abiding" in the Lord's presence, peace, and guidance, and of Him "abiding" in us through the Holy Spirit.

We know from this scripture that in this abiding space we are the most spiritually productive, "bearing much fruit." Who doesn't want that?! I know I do. I also find that when I'm in close communion with the Lord through prayer, listening, and reading His Word, I'm at my most peaceful, and my faith rises. Our Creator wired us, so He knows what we most need, which is to be connected to Him. In this song I talk about stopping to dwell in the moment and space we're in, focusing on our communion with God. I invite you to do so now.

Questions

- What does "remaining in" the Lord mean to you?
- The fact that we have protection available under the Lord's spiritual covering is such a marvelous miracle. How do you connect to this action of remaining in the Lord and taking refuge in His covering when you're feeling worried or scared?

- I bear much better fruit when I remain close to the Lord. When I don't, my faith wanes and my patience is thin. Have you noticed this for yourself? Can you think of any recent examples?
- How does this song's painting speak to you?

Prayer

Lord, I want to stay connected to You and bear good fruit. I want my heart to be Your home. When so many distractions pull for my attention, help me remain in You. In Jesus' name, amen..

5
Spirit of God

Kim Gentry Meyer

Spirit of God

by Kim Gentry Meyer

Verse 1

Spirit of God
Speak to our spirit
Come testify
We belong to You
Come testify
Come testify
Come testify
Spirit of God

Verse 2

Spirit of God
You know our weakness
Your prayers for us
Go beyond words
Come pray for us
Come pray for us
Come pray for us
Spirit of God

Chorus

Poured out on us
To show the Father's love
Spirit of Truth
We worship You

Verse 3

Spirit of God
We love Your presence
Come fill us now
With more of You
Come fill us now
Come fill us now
Come fill us now
Spirit of God

Anchor scriptures

- Romans 8:16 The Spirit himself testifies with our spirit that we are God's children.
- Romans 8:26 ... the Spirit helps us in our weakness. We do not know what we ought to pray for, but the Spirit himself intercedes for us through wordless groans.
- Acts 4:31 After they prayed, the place where they were meeting was shaken. And they were all filled with the Holy Spirit and spoke the word of God boldly.
- Acts 2:17 ... I will pour out my Spirit on all people.
- John 14:16–17 And I will ask the Father, and he will give you another advocate to help you and be with you forever—the Spirit of truth...
- John 4:24 God is spirit, and his worshipers must worship in the Spirit and in truth.

Reflection

Embracing the full Trinity can seem hard to comprehend. That's why I felt strongly called to write a song about the roles, work, and personhood of the Holy Spirit in a more substantive way than your typical song on this topic. Each section is tied to specific Bible scriptures, so the song packs a real punch from a content perspective!

In addition, the song is sung directly to the Holy Spirit, so it is a heart cry of sorts. For example, Verse 1 asks Him to directly speak to our spirit (Romans 8:16), and Verse 2 asks Him to pray for us when we don't have the words (Romans 8:26). Then in Verse 3 I cover the narrative you hear more commonly in worship songs: asking His presence to come fill us (Acts 4:31).

For the Chorus, I wanted to celebrate that the Holy Spirit is given as a gift, and also to proclaim He is the Spirit of Truth (John 14:16–17; John 4:24).

This is an upbeat song meant to celebrate the Holy Spirit's work in our lives and bring joy to all who hear it. I certainly hope you find that to be true.

Questions

- Which lyrics do you connect with the most? Why?
- Sometimes I forget that the Holy Spirit has such a multifaceted role in our lives. Are any of these scriptural illustrations new or surprising to you? If so, which one(s)?
- How does this song's painting speak to you?

Prayer

Lord, thank You for the gift of the Holy Spirit as a comforter, advocate, Truth teller, and so much more. I want to embrace this part of the Trinity fully and walk with the Spirit all my days. Empower me to do so, and to share the fullness of God with others. In Jesus' name, amen.

6

Perfect Love

Perfect Love

by Kim Gentry Meyer

Verse 1

Perfect love
You found me again
You chased me down around dark corners of my heart
And where I end
My hope begins
You see the good in me when all I see is failure

Chorus

How high and
How wide
Is Your love for me

Verse 2

Perfect love
You bridged the gap
You made a way for me to be with You forever
And here I stand
Because of grace
Not because of anything I could have done

Bridge

There is no fear in Your love
There is no holding back of mercy
I find freedom in Your love
You gave Your life to save me
Now I'm free

Anchor scriptures

- Ephesians 3:17–19 And I pray that you, being rooted and established in love, may have power, together with all the Lord's holy people, to grasp how wide and long and high and deep is the love of Christ, and to know this love that surpasses knowledge—that you may be filled to the measure of all the fullness of God.
- 1 John 4:18 There is no fear in love. But perfect love drives out fear, because fear has to do with punishment. The one who fears is not made perfect in love.
- John 3:16 For God so loved the world that he gave his one and only Son, that whoever believes in him shall not perish but have eternal life.

Reflection

I wrote this song for an Easter service, as a simple way to explain the gospel to family members and friends who might be visiting and not familiar with it. You'll see that Verse 2 and the Bridge really spell that out. But this song has evolved into much more than that for me. I especially identify with Verse 1. I'm continually amazed that Jesus pursues me and helps me when I feel like I'm in a dark corner. This verse is right up there with "Mind of Christ" as a tool I use to stand firmly in the love of God and the renewal of my mind. I hope this song helps you too.

Questions

- Loving perfectly is beyond our ability or comprehension. But we can lean into what the Bible says about God's perfect love (see anchor scriptures), and that gives us a lot to go on! Is this idea of God's perfect love for you comforting? Surprising? Does it seem near or distant? Why?

- The Chorus of this song describes the measure of His love for us, and the Verses and Bridge describe the actions of His love. I find that different parts of the song stand out to me depending on what I'm going through at the time. Which part of this song stands out to you most right now? Why?
- I address the topic of fear in the Bridge, because even though it can be such a challenging emotion to manage, 1 John 4:18 reminds us that perfect love drives out fear. How does this make you feel? Hopeful? Peaceful? What else?
- How does this song's painting speak to you?

Prayer

Father, thank You for Your perfect and endless love for me, paid for at the highest price through Jesus' sacrifice. Thank You for chasing me down even when I reject Your love and don't feel worthy of it. Deepen my revelation of Your perfect love so I can stand more firmly in it and find greater freedom in it. I celebrate the fact that fear cannot stand against Your perfect love and that peace flows from it. I receive all of this in Jesus' name, amen.

7

We Surrender to Love

We Surrender to Love

by Kim Gentry Meyer and Adam Russell

Verse

Let the peace of God
That passes worldly knowing
Come and fill us to the point of overflowing
As we surrender to Your love

Holy Spirit come revive this generation
And restore to us the joy of our salvation
As we surrender to Your love
Father, Spirit, Son

Chorus

In repentance we have come
We are drawn in by Your love
We surrender

There's a change we need to make
And a turn we need to take
We surrender
We surrender to love

Bridge

We're ready for a new thing
We're believing for a new thing
We're ready for a new thing
In You

We're leaving fear behind us
Holding on to what You've promised
We're ready for a new thing
In You

Anchor scriptures

- Philippians 4:7 And the peace of God, which transcends all understanding, will guard your hearts and your minds in Christ Jesus.
- Romans 15:13 May the God of hope fill you with all joy and peace as you trust in him, so that you may overflow with hope by the power of the Holy Spirit.
- Psalm 51:12 Restore to me the joy of your salvation and grant me a willing spirit, to sustain me.
- Psalm 85:6 Will you not revive us again, that your people may rejoice in you?
- 2 Peter 3:9 The Lord is not slow in keeping his promise, as some understand slowness. Instead he is patient with you, not wanting anyone to perish, but everyone to come to repentance.
- Isaiah 43:19 See, I am doing a new thing! Now it springs up; do you not perceive it? I am making a way in the wilderness and streams in the wasteland.
- 2 Timothy 1:7 For the Spirit God gave us does not make us timid, but gives us power, love and self-discipline.
- Psalm 51:10 Create in me a pure heart, O God, and renew a steadfast spirit within me.

Reflection

My goal with this song is to present repentance (Chorus) in a way that is encouraging and empowering, because it should be! I believe it's a game changer when we shift our thinking about repentance in a way that celebrates it as an expression of God's love and integrates it more deeply into daily life. The doors to revival (second part of the Verse) are opened when we repent and turn ourselves back to the Lord (Chorus). Only then can He do the "new thing" (Bridge). The forgiveness we are gifted through repentance, paid for at the highest price by Christ, is just that...a gift. Why wouldn't we want to access this gift more fully?

In the Chorus I talk about how there needs to be a turning after repentance; repentance alone is not enough. If we don't make a change, we will end up back where we were, and the cycle will repeat. This view of repentance is unpopular in an age where so many believe there is no absolute right or wrong and instead follow their "own truth," as I discussed in Chapter 1. I for one am thankful for Biblical truth and the privilege of repentance, which is a loving gift from our Heavenly Father that offers us a way back into full relationship with Him and aligns us with His will for our lives.

Questions

- We all want the "new thing," but are we willing to move forward for it (Bridge)? Are we ready to repent and turn, leaving fear behind us and letting go of the old? I know this sometimes trips me up. I must be willing to step out and look forward. What "new thing(s)" do you desire? Do you identify anything holding you back?
- Does the topic of repentance feel unpleasant to think about and awkward to talk about? Why? How does this song help you shift your thinking about repentance?
- How does this song's painting speak to you?

Prayer

Father, sometimes I resist repentance, even though it is a precious gift and is necessary to walk in greater freedom and power with You. Help me recognize and deal with the areas where I need to repent and make a change. I really do desire a "new thing" and a greater work of Your hand on my life, my family, my ministry, and my broader community. Thank You for always meeting me with open arms when I surrender to Your love and Your ways. In Jesus' name, amen."

8

Full Circle

Full Circle

by Kim Gentry Meyer

Verse 1

I think I've almost come around
And I can lay my troubles down
It's funny how a circle always stops where it starts
And every little season has a place in the heart
Like a patchwork quilt
Memories cover me until
There is peace
Oh-oh-oh-oh, oh
Oh-oh-oh-oh, o-o-oh

Verse 2

Sometimes you win, sometimes you lose
And sometimes you don't get to choose
Life throws you some curve balls, you just go with the flow
Hit the ones you can and then just let the rest go
Enjoy the game, having some fun along the way
Then go home
Oh-oh-oh-oh, oh
Oh-oh-oh-oh, o-o-h

Verse 3

Oh, oh, oh it's time to go
I hear the Father call me home
We all make our choices
And I have made mine
I'm secure in knowing
Where my hope lies
My race is run
All is said and done
Now, goodbye

Anchor scriptures

- Jeremiah 17:7 But blessed is the one who trusts in the Lord, whose confidence is in him.
- Psalm 33:20 We wait in hope for the lord; he is our help and our shield.
- 1 Peter 3:15 But in your hearts revere Christ as Lord. Always be prepared to give an answer to everyone who asks you to give the reason for the hope that you have....
- Hebrews 12:1–2 ... let us throw off everything that hinders and the sin that so easily entangles. And let us run with perseverance the race marked out for us, fixing our eyes on Jesus, the pioneer and perfecter of faith....
- 2 Timothy 4:7 I have fought the good fight, I have finished the race, I have kept the faith.

Reflection

My purpose for this song is twofold: to prompt people to think about where their hope lies (Verse 3) and to be a comfort and encouragement to believers who are approaching the end of this life. We shy away from talking about death, when as believers we can celebrate what is to come after. I wanted to try to put myself in someone's shoes who is going through the process of making peace with dying (Verses 1–2) and then comes to a place of peace and is at rest as they go on to be with the Lord (Verse 3). I pray this song will be healing to both those who are nearing the end of life and also to their loved ones.

Questions

- What part of this song stands out most for you?

- There is great comfort in knowing where our hope lies, yet this topic can still be very uncomfortable. Why do you think that is? I encourage you to meditate on the comfort of salvation and the peace that comes with the hope we have.
- How does this song's painting speak to you?

Prayer

Lord, thank You for being our hope. Thank You for salvation. Help me replace the fear of death with the comfort of Your promises. And help me share this hope with those around me so that they can also know where their hope lies. In Jesus' name, amen.

About the Artist

Kim's latest music project, *Herald*, honors her folk-pop roots while incorporating diverse sonic elements. Released through NWN Records and Integrated Music Rights, part of the Integrity Music family, it features eight original songs rooted in Scripture, with her gentle vocals and folk-pop style enhanced by producer and co-writer Karl Anderson. *Herald* carries themes of restoration, peace, and hope throughout, all anchored in Kim's desire to be a herald for the Lord.

And now this companion book, *Herald Reflections*, melds Kim's musical and visual artistic gifts with her strong writing ability to give praise and honor to God and encouragement to others.

Beyond the music, Meyer, a visual artist in the impressionist/expressionist tradition, personally painted not only the beautiful artwork for the *Herald* album cover and *Herald Reflections* book cover, but the eight individual sunset pieces found in *Herald Reflections*; one to accompany each track on the album. "The sunsets signify the whole idea of being a herald to proclaim the coming of the Lord," she reveals.

As a music artist, Kim has performed at noted venues in Nashville and Austin and received numerous awards and recognitions. She holds a bachelor's degree in business and a master's degree in social work and is a professional fundraiser whose proposals have raised over $25 million for various nonprofit organizations.

She was recently named a 2023 Woody Guthrie Poet and was invited to read her newly published poem, "You'll Find Me There" (which appears in song form on her new *Herald* album) during the 2023 Woody Guthrie Folk Festival, which celebrates the life and work of the late legendary singer/songwriter best known for his song, "This Land is Your Land."

As a former Mrs. Massachusetts America, Kim is passionate about community service. She and her husband Adam have been involved with animal rescue efforts for over 20 years and have fostered over 100 dogs and cats. They currently make their home on Cape Cod with their houseful of rescued pets.